ANIMAL LIVES

The Otter

KINGFISHER
Larousse Kingfisher Chambers Inc.
95 Madison Avenue
New York, New York 10016

First published in 1999
2 4 6 8 10 9 7 5 3 1
1(TR)/0299/SC/RPR(NEW)/150NYM

LIBRARY OF CONGRESS CATALOGING-IN-PUBLICATION DATA
Ransford, Sandy.
The otter / Sandy Ransford; Bert Kitchen, illustrator. — 1st ed.
p. cm. — (Animal lives)
Includes index.
Summary: Describes how otters construct their homes, find food,
mate, play, and care for their young.
1. Lutra lutra — Juvenile literature. [1. Otters.] I. Kitchen,
Bert, ill. II. Title. III. Series: Animal lives (New York, N.Y.)
QL737.C25R25 1999
599.769'2 — dc21 98–40378 CIP AC

Series editor: Miranda Smith
Series designer: Sarah Goodwin

ISBN 0-7534-5176-X

Printed in Hong Kong

ANIMAL LIVES

The Otter

Illustrated by
Bert Kitchen

Written by
Sandy Ransford

KING*f*ISHER

NEW YORK

As the shadows lengthen and the day draws to its close, a sleek brown animal slips silently from its hole in the riverbank. The otter is off to hunt for food. Taking a deep breath, and closing her ears and nostrils to keep out the water, she dives. Powerful, web-footed hind legs propel her swiftly forward; her strong, thick tail steers. She stays under for about half a minute, then comes up to breathe.

Fast as an arrow, slippery as an eel, the otter shoots through the water, twisting and turning after her prey. Although hunting is a serious business, she seems to swim for sheer joy. Fish, eels, frogs, voles— even ducklings and coots— make up her supper. Her speed lets her sneak up on them without warning. She eats smaller creatures under water, but carries the larger ones ashore.

❧ 6 ❧

So lithe and graceful in the water, the otter moves clumsily on land. With her long body arching upward, she waddles like a duck, dragging her tail along the ground. She shakes the water out of her coat; tiny droplets sparkle in the moonlight. Then she settles down to eat a large eel, one of her favorite foods. Because it is slippery, she holds it between her forepaws as she chews. After her meal, she will groom herself, like a cat. Grooming spreads oil from her skin through the fur, to help keep her coat waterproof.

**W**hether on land or in the water, the otter is always on the lookout for danger. People and dogs are especially threatening. At the slightest hint of someone approaching—the snap of a brittle twig, a rustling in the grass—she will slip silently into the water, bolt for her hole, or if it is too far away, hide in the nearby undergrowth. She has caught a strange scent in the air, so to get a good look, she rears up, propping herself up with her tail. But this time it is not danger that approaches, but another otter. It is a young male, seeking a mate. For most of the year otters live alone. But the droppings and scent they leave behind act as messages to other otters. A female otter's droppings can tell a male that she is ready to breed. When he detects this, he will track her down.

T he two otters meet, then tumble together into the water and start to play, chasing fish and ducks and each other, diving and somersaulting, twisting and turning, spiraling around and around each other with delight. They will romp together like this for several hours, playing both in and out of the water. It is their way of getting to know and trust each other, so they can become mates.

The otters leap from the water and bound along the riverbank, chasing each other and playing tag. The female stops for a moment to shake droplets of glistening river water out of her coat; the male joins her, then the two otters roll on the grass to dry themselves. Their thick, wet fur reflects the light, helping them to take on the appearance of their surroundings, and making them difficult to spot. But they pause for only a few moments before resuming their play, racing up and down, pouncing on each other and rolling over, then rushing off again. Once they have gotten to know each other really well, the two otters will become mates. The female signals to the male that she is ready to accept him as a mate by rolling over on her back with her paws in the air.

At dawn, the female otter swims home. Her holt might be a hole in a riverbank, or between rocks on a quiet coastline. It has two entrances, one under water, so she can come and go without being seen. She lives alone most of the year, traveling each night in search of food, sleeping each day in a different holt. Even though she now has a mate, the two spend their days apart.

For nine weeks, baby cubs grow inside the female otter. She digs a special holt, hidden far away from danger, and lines it with grass and reeds. Here, her cubs are born. There are two cubs, although there could be as many as four. Tiny, blind, and helpless, they stay close to their mother, drinking her milk and snuggling up to her for warmth. Their short, soft baby fur doesn't provide much protection. Several days pass before she leaves them, even for a short time, to look for food. Instead, her mate brings her fish.

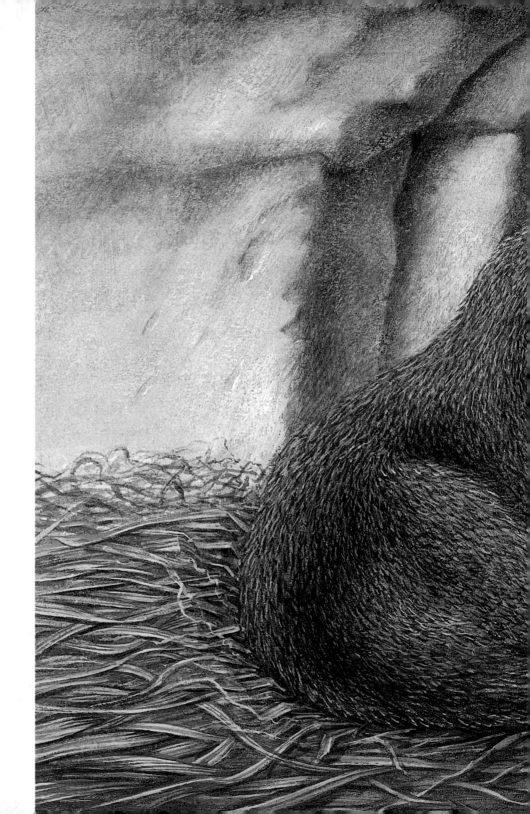

When they are a month old, the cubs' eyes open and they see the world around them for the first time. A few weeks later they take their first fumbling steps and begin to explore. But their little legs don't always do what they want them to! They still drink their mother's milk, but now she leaves them for short periods to hunt, and brings them back pieces of half-chewed fish.

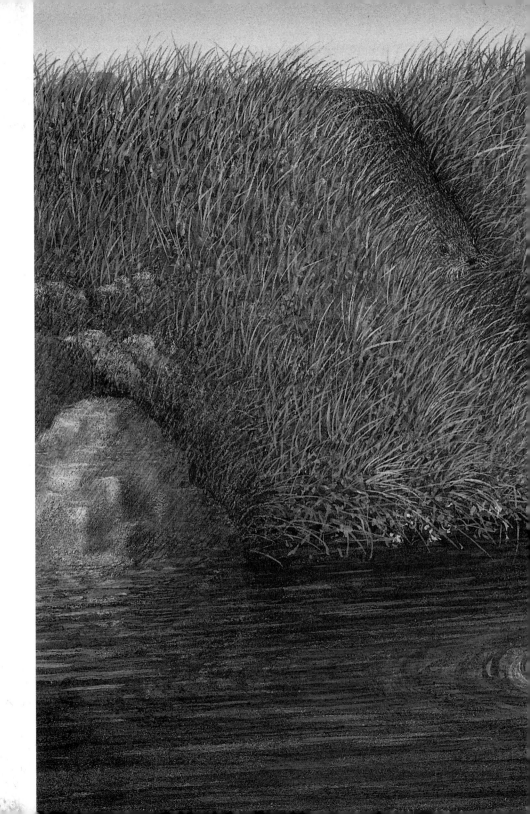

One day, when the cubs are about three months old, their mother nudges them out of the holt and introduces them to the water. The shimmering darkness is terrifying to the little otters. Timidly, they watch her dive in. Then one cub glides down the riverbank to join her, and the other follows. The cubs flounder around at first, but soon they are dog-paddling along the surface.

The cubs soon feel at home in the river. One hitches a ride on her mother's back; the other swims behind her. They all have fun, playing in the water. Once they are confident, it is time to learn how to dive. Their mother takes them out to deeper water. It is cold, and the cubs are scared. She grabs one by the scruff of his neck and pulls him three feet under before releasing him. Terrified, the other cub heads for the bank, but she cannot escape her turn. The cubs must dive in order to feed themselves. For their first lesson, their mother catches a small fish, and gives it to them to kill. Then she releases another fish in front of them, so they can learn how to catch it for themselves. Before long, the otter cubs will be diving and hunting on their own.

The male otter stays with his family for only a few days after the cubs are born, bringing food to his mate. He then returns to his solitary life. About a year after their birth the cubs will also leave their mother. When they are gone, she lives alone, hunting by night and sleeping by day, until the time comes to find another mate and bring up another family.

THE RIVER OTTER

Name: The river otter or North American otter; scientific name: *Lutra canadensis*.

Family: All otters are members of the animal family called *Mustelidae*, which includes stoats, weasels, polecats, and pine martens.

Size: Male river otters measure up to 4 feet from head to tail. The females measure up to 3.5 feet.

Weight: Males weigh up to 25 pounds. Females weigh up to 16 pounds.

Distribution: Found across much of North America. Populations have declined since the 1960s, but have increased again in recent years.

Habitat: Remote rivers and coastlines in wild places unlikely to be disturbed by people.

Prey: Fish, eels, frogs, shellfish; also small voles, birds, and ducklings.

Nests: Called holts, usually holes in the riverbank among tree roots or under rocky ledges.

Young: Usually two cubs are born in late winter or early spring.

Other species: The Eurasian otter, which is very similar to the river otter; the giant otter of Brazil, which may be up to 7 feet long and is now very rare; the oriental small-clawed otter, which is the smallest in the world; the clawless otter; the sea otter; the smooth-coated otter; the hairy-nosed otter.

OTTER DISTRIBUTION

Otters are found on every continent except Australia and Antarctica. They were once common, but nowadays they are quite rare, because they have been hunted for their fur and to stop them taking fish. Many have been poisoned by pesticides that find their way into rivers and then into the small fish on which the otters feed. However, in recent years the water quality of some rivers has improved, and otters are gradually making a comeback in some parts of the world.

HOW TO WATCH OTTERS

Otters are shy, elusive animals that live in remote places with few inhabitants. Look for single rocks or promontories, and check them for otter droppings, which are called spraints. Grayish in color, these contain a lot of fish bones, and if you find any, you can be sure that there are otters around. To spot an otter, you must be prepared to wait a long time without moving, hidden behind a bank, bush, or rock so you do not stand out against the skyline. Dress in dark clothes and speak only in low whispers. You may be rewarded with the sight of an otter. Do not disturb it! When you have had your fill of looking, quietly creep away.

OTTER WORDS

coat an animal's fur

cub a baby or young otter

elusive difficult to spot

holt an otter's home, usually a hole in the riverbank

hunt chase an animal for food

lithe slender and flexible

mate male or female partner

pesticide poison sprayed on crops to kill insects

prey an animal that is killed for food

promontory a piece of land or rock that juts out into water

scent distinctive smell of an animal

scruff of the neck loose skin at the back of an animal's neck

solitary living alone

spraint an otter's droppings

web-footed having toes joined by pieces of skin, like a duck

FOR FURTHER INFORMATION

International Wildlife Education and Conservation
237 Hill Street
Santa Monica, CA 90405
(310) 392 6257
www.iwec.org

Otternet
www.otternet.com

International Otter Survival Fund
iosf@otter.org
www.otter.org

River Otter Alliance
6733 South Locust Court
Englewood, CO 80112

INDEX

ACKNOWLEDGMENTS

The author and publishers are grateful for the help and advice that Philip Wayre of the Otter Trust has given them in the preparation of this book, and thank Muriel Kitchen and Sergio Ransford for the photographs on the jacket.